To Gra...
Christmas, 1983

Jon

The World of
CATS

The World of
CATS

Angela Sayer

NEW YORK

Photography by Angela Sayer
(Colour Library International front and back covers,
endpapers; Bruce Coleman – Hans Reinhard, frontispiece)

Contents

History, Myth and Folklore

The cat is a relative newcomer to the company of man and is unique in that it is the only animal universally accepted in a domesticated role for strictly non-utilitarian purposes. Although the domestic feline is an efficient controller of small rodents and other vermin, it was probably after the animal's acceptance as a camp follower and convenient scavenger that this trait was discovered. Indeed it may well have been the preponderance of rats and mice around settlements that encouraged the cat's first timorous approach.

The typical independence of the feline prevents the cat from ever becoming the same sort of pet as the servile, adoring dog and, even today, the cat:man relationship exists on strictly feline terms.

Cats took over from other small and often vicious animals in the guarding of the granaries of Ancient Egypt about 5000 years ago, and soon became popular as house pets, too, for they were thought to ward off evil as well as being killers of vermin and snakes. Most of the tomb paintings, frescoes and cat ornaments of those times show the cat as a small sleek tabby-patterned creature and, like many other animals of the Egyptians, it soon became deified. The cat was sacred to the goddess Pasht or Bastet, and it may well be from the first of these two names that our own word 'puss' is derived. It is quite possible that the cat was domesticated as a house pet in India at about the same time as it was accepted in Egypt, but Sanscrit writings make only a few references to cats, while the Egyptians left an invaluable legacy of feline history, recording the cat in all its moods and postures, and in all manner of situations. Tiny cat figures were made in all materials from clay to gold, and were often pierced so that they could be worn as amulets. Other ornaments were made of mother cats and their litters of kittens, nursing or playing around their feet in family groups.

A cat cult was established and a great red granite temple was raised to the glory of Bastet at Beni Hassan on the banks of the Nile. When a pet cat died the

The cat of Ancient Egypt was generally tabby in pattern, and with long, svelte lines.

Egyptian family would go into mourning and shave off their eyebrows as a mark of respect. Even the poorest of people would spend as much as they could afford on having the animal embalmed, and then the small body was taken in procession to its burial ground accompanied by the bereft family, beating gongs and wailing. Great cat cemeteries have been excavated and over 300 000 mummified cats were discovered at the Beni Hassan site alone.

When Cambyses, son of Cyrus the Great of Persia, attacked the port of Peluse he used the Egyptians' love of cats to his own advantage. He ordered his front line of troops to carry live cats as they marched on the fortress, and his ploy worked. Rather than risk killing any of the sacred animals, the Egyptians capitulated, and Cambyses won a unique, bloodless victory.

The precious cats of the Ancient Egyptians gradually made their way, by means of the great trade routes, to other parts of the world, often to be kept in palaces and temples but never again afforded quite such reverence as in the days of Bastet. The Egyptians had called their cat 'mau', a word that meant 'to see', and this name was retained, or changed to 'mao' by the peoples of both Ancient China and Japan when they first adopted cats and took them into their homes. It was the Romans, however, who augmented the worldwide distribution of the domestic cat, for in the wake of their invincible legions, the cat spread across Europe and eventually to the Western world.

There are many towns and villages throughout the world with feline connotations to their names. For example, the old stronghold of Cat Vicense in Holland, first named by the Romans, is now called Kattewyk or 'Cat's Town', and there are many other similar cases. The Romans probably brought cats to Britain, but others were certainly introduced by Phoenician sea traders and exchanged for commodities such as tin from the Cornish

Below: A modern 'Egyptian' kitten, *Chocind Hussar*, poses with a bronze Bastet figurine.

Bottom: Today's reconstructed cats of Egyptian type are called Oriental Spotteds, and these playful examples are called *Solitaire Sekhmet* and *Selene*.

Samantha hunts in the tall grass. Although her red colouring is striking to our eyes, most animals see red and green as similar shades, therefore she would be camouflaged.

mines and other goods. Humans all over the world were quick to recognize the value of the cat in keeping down pests, especially in the vital corn stores, and by the year 936 King Howell the Good of Wales included the protection of the cat in his New Laws. Severe penalties and fines were imposed on anyone stealing or killing a cat, its full value depending upon its age, size and hunting abilities. Protected and respected, the cat prospered, and became established as part of man's family and life. It's value was enhanced further when returning Crusaders unwittingly brought back virulent disease, spread by the rats which infested their ships, but despite the efforts of the rat-catching cats, the Black Death raged through all the civilized lands of Europe taking a dreadful toll of human life. The Crusaders also brought treasures home from the East, including strange and beautiful cats discovered during their travels, some of which had long silky fur.

During the Middle Ages, feline fortunes were reversed. The cat had played a prominent part in a cult which had sprung up in the Rhinelands. Freya,

goddess of fertility and the harvest, traditionally rode in a chariot drawn by two cats, and cats were featured in the rejoicing and rites. The Church in Europe initiated counterattacks to such ceremonies which gathered momentum and culminated in the institution of horrendous witch-hunts throughout North and West Europe.

Pope Innocent VIII and the Inquisition legalized the persecution of witches, linking the cat with the Devil, and thousands of innocent people were tortured and put to death along with their cats. This terrible orgy of killing reached peaks on Saint Days, when ritual burnings took place, and witch-hunting spread to England and even across the Atlantic to New England.

The mass destruction of cats, which accompanied the taking of thousands of human lives, resulted in an enormous increase in the rat population. Plague and pestilence soon followed the wave of witch-hunts. The first witchcraft trial took place in Europe during the 13th century and the last occurred in Scotland in 1722.

Eventually sanity returned to the world and the cat settled down to its role of indispensable companion and highly valued worker and its numbers increased again accordingly.

The first cat imported into Paraguay in 1750 was purchased for a pound weight of gold, and during the Californian Gold Rush cats brought from Europe also commanded very high prices. The tide had turned at last and the cat was restored to favour. Cats quickly became the favourites of the famous, and distinctive types and breeds began to emerge. More ordinary cats quietly went about the business on farms and ships, in town and country, keeping the rodent population under control once more.

Today, there are domestic cats in every corner of the world. Some have long authenticated pedigrees while others have no recorded ancestry whatever. Some have long silky coats, some short sleek pelts. Some live in luxury in palatial homes, others spend their lives in barns and farm buildings. But whatever its circumstances, the cat is a survivor and one which has truly benefited from its unique spirit of independence.

All of the cat's features are designed to make it an efficient hunter and a successful product of evolution.

This cat makes use of a natural vantage-point from which to watch and wait for suitable prey.

Long-haired Cats

During the 16th century the first long-coated cats were brought out of Angora, now called Ankara, in Turkey. They were transported first to France and then to Britain and were greatly prized for the beauty of their unusual coats. Though many of these Angora cats were white, a learned contemporary writer, enthralled

Similar to some of the very first long-haired cats from the East, this Turkish Angora has odd-eye colour.

by the creatures, wrote of them as being 'Ash-colored, Dun and Speckled Cats, beautiful to behold'.

Soon after the discovery of the Turkish long-hairs, more long-coated cats were brought from Persia, now known as Iran. These were of a different build to the Angoras, having heavier, stockier body conformation and the hair was fluffy in contrast to the silky fur of the Angora.

Unfortunately, very little written information has survived regarding the fortunes of the long-haired cats from their introduction to the West until the 19th century, when Chatles H. Ross astounded his friends by producing a book of cats. He described the Angora cat of the 1860s as a beautiful variety with silvery, silken hair, longest on the neck and tail, and some as being almost the colour of the lion. Mr. Ross wrote of the Persian cat as having very long hair of a uniform grey colour, and as being even more beautiful than the Angora. To both varieties he attributed gentle manners. By the end of the 19th century the first cat shows had been held in Britain and the United States of America, and cats were being selectively bred for both type and colour. Breeders began to keep records of matings, and these eventually constituted pedigrees. The interbreeding between the Angora and Persian cats caused the more dominant characteristics to prevail and gradually the heavier and more densely coated Persian type took over to become the accepted long-haired show cat.

As more and more fanciers became interested in cats, clubs and societies were formed. These, in turn, organized regular shows and exhibitions, judges were appointed and the first registrations of litters were entered. By the year 1901 the selection of long-haired cats officially recognized included Black, White, Blue, Orange Cream and Sable in solid-coloured varieties plus Smoke, Chinchilla, Tabby, Tortoiseshell, Bi-coloured and Tri-coloured.

Modern long-haired varieties have been carefully bred to conform to very exacting standards and, on the show bench, each cat is judged against its own breed requirements.

THE PERSIAN CAT TODAY

The pedigree Persian of today must have a round massive head, very broad across the skull with rounded underlying bone structure. The ears should be very small with curved tips, set far apart and fitting into the general rounded contour of the head. The Persian's eyes should be very large, round and set wide apart. The full

Above: Still very young, this Blue Persian is showing transitional eyecolour between the blue of babyhood and the copper of the adult.

Left: Most Persian cats are required to have copper eyes, like this lovely White.

11

Right: A young Black Persian kitten enjoys his first outing in the spring sunshine.

Below: Most popular of all the Persians is the Blue, with its sound coloured coat and deep copper eyes.

cheeks, firm chin and short snub nose all add to the chunky look of the appealing face. Cats of this type must have cobby bodies with short thick legs and large round paws. The head is supported on a short strong neck and the tail is short, but in proportion to the length of the body.

It is the coat, however, which makes the cat a Persian. It is long and so thick that it stands away from the body disguising the animal's contours. The hair texture is fine and it has a healthy glossy appearance. Around the neck there should be a ruff or frill of extra-long hair which continues between the front legs; there should be long tufts on the ears and between the toes. The tail is also well furnished with extra-long hair. Known as a 'brush', it should be carried straight and slightly lower than the line of the spine.

Persians come in assorted and very beautiful colours, and different governing bodies throughout the world recognize different colours and patterns.

Solid-Coloured Persians The U.S.A.'s largest and foremost registering body is the Cat Fanciers' Association Incorporated and it accepts solid-coloured Persians in Black, White, Blue, Red and

Cream. The Black Persian must be a dense coal-black right through its coat from the roots to the tips, and is penalized on the show bench for having any rust-coloured markings or light hair in the undercoat. Its paw pads and nose leather should be black, too, and its eyes a brilliant copper.

The White Persian must be a pure glistening white all over without a single dark hair of any colour. Its nose leather and paw pads are pink and it may have eyes of either deep blue or brilliant copper. There are Odd-Eyed White Persians too, in which one eye is blue and the other is copper.

Blue Persians are among the oldest of all the varieties and are still the most popular. Although any shade of blue is allowed, the lighter shades are preferred by judges, but whatever the coat tone, it must be totally sound in intensity from nose tip to tail. Blue Persians have deep copper eyes.

Red Persian cats are difficult to breed to top show standard as the deep, rich, red coat should not show any shadings, markings or ticking, or any light areas at the lips or chin. With its brick-red nose leather and copper eyes, an exhibition Red Persian is a rare, magnificent sight.

Cream Persians must be evenly coloured a light buff shade and have nose leather and paw pads of a light pink shade. The copper eye-colour adds great impact to the delicately coloured face. Like all the solid-coloured cats, the Cream loses points for showing any ghostly tabby markings in its coat or having light or green-tinged eyes.

Here we can clearly see the contrast between the Red and Cream Persian coat colouring, one being the dilute version of the other.

13

Silcresta Daren is a young Chinchilla with typical film-star appeal.

Multi-coloured Persians There are so many patterned varieties of Persians that it is usual to discuss them in groups, such as the TABBIES, the TORTIES, the SMOKES and so on, but there is one breed which stands alone and has been recognized for almost one hundred years. The CHINCHILLA is a veritable filmstar of a cat and is popularly used in all types of modelling and advertising. Its undercoat is pure white but each hair on the head, back, sides and tail has a black tip, which gives the cat its characteristically sparkling, silvered appearance. The Chinchilla's emerald or aquamarine eyes are dramatically outlined with black, and distinctive brick-red nose leather adds to its exotic look. More heavily marked with black, so that the cat appears to wear a dark mantle, is the Shaded Silver, another beauty with similar eye colour. In Britain there are two almost identical breeds, one also called the Shaded Silver with sea-green eyes, and another known as the Pewter, which has orange- or copper-coloured eyes.

Rare indeed is the Chinchilla Golden, bred from kittens which appeared by chance in regular Chinchilla litters. This cat has a warm cream undercoat and the hairs of the head, back, sides and tail are just tipped with seal brown, which gives an unusual golden aura to the coat. The cat's underparts, chest, chin and distinctive ear-tufts are cream. The emerald or aquamarine eyes, the rose-coloured nose and the lips are sharply defined by seal-brown outlines. Similar, but more heavily shaded with seal brown (analogous to the Shaded Silver), is the Shaded Golden.

When red and silver genes were mixed together in long-haired cats, the resulting cocktail produced the CAMEO series of unusual and very eye-catching Persians.

The Shell Cameo or Red Chinchilla is basically white with the hair tips coloured light red. This gives a sparkling pink-tinged glow to the cat. The ear-tufts and chest are white and the nose-leather, eye-rims and paw pads are rose pink. Like all cats in this group, the huge, lustrous eyes are a brilliant copper colour. The Shaded Cameo or Red-Shaded cats look considerably darker than the Shell because the white undercoat is overlaid with a distinctive mantle of red tipping. There are Shell and Shaded Tortoiseshell cats, too, in which the tipping and the mantle respectively, are randomly patched with red and black. Such cats should ideally have a red- or cream-tipped blaze bisecting the face, and are very pretty indeed.

Darkest in the group is the CAMEO RED or RED SMOKE. In fact this variety is so heavily tipped with red that it may look like a red long-haired cat until it moves, when the white undercoat may be seen rippling under the red over-hairs. The neck frill and ear-tufts are white too, features which typify Smoke cats of other colours as well.

Rare and beautiful, this Shaded Golden is a cousin of the Shaded Silver, but with golden brown tipping.

Left: *Toanje Blossom*, a Shaded Cameo, is an example of the combined effect of red and silver genes.

15

The BLACK SMOKE, known as the 'cat of contrasts' and bred for more than a hundred years, is a massive and majestic animal. Its white undercoat shows through the black topcoat as it moves, and its full ruff or frill and ear-tufts of silvery-white give a startlingly contrasting effect. There is a dilute variety of this cat, too, called the Blue Smoke. The dilution gene reduces the black coloration to a blue-grey, while the undercoat, frill and ear-tufts remain very white.

TABBY PERSIANS are delightful and come in two patterns, known as the Classic and the Mackerel, as well as in several attractive colours.

The Classic pattern has dense and deeply defined dark markings on a lighter base coat, and for show purposes, these markings must conform to set designs. The cat's legs must be evenly banded with bracelets and the tail must have even rings along its length. The neck should have several clear and unbroken necklaces. On the head, dark frown lines form an intricate 'M' on the forehead, and dark lines run back from the outer corners of the eyes. On the body the markings should form the shape of a butterfly draped across the cat's shoulders, while identical whorls with inner dots should be etched on both of the animal's sides. Long, dark lines run from the 'butterfly' to the tail and the underparts have two rows of spots, rather like vest buttons.

In the Mackerel, the legs, head and tail have similar markings to the Classic, but instead of the intricate swirls and whorls, narrow lines of dark colour run straight from the spine line vertically down the body.

Silver Tabby Persians have clear silver coats with dense black markings, while the Brown Tabby's black markings are defined against a coppery brown base coat. In the Blue Tabby deep blue-grey mark-

Champion *Oxus Tarquinius Superbus*, an aptly named Black Smoke male.

Left and below: *Kedong Tana*, a Silver Tabby, stands demurely to show her classic markings . . . before proceeding to take time to wash her paws and face.

ings with a warm fawn overtone cover a ground colour of bluish ivory. The Red Tabby's pattern consists of a deep rich red on a paler red coat, while the Cream Tabby is much paler, being buff or cream on a very pale cream base coat. The Cameo Tabby is very pretty, with an off-white coat showing the tabby pattern in light red.

PATCHED TABBIES, sometimes called TORBIES, can be strikingly marked. The Torbie is an established Silver, Brown or Blue Tabby with additional patches of red or cream, hence its name which is derived from Tortoiseshell-Tabby.

All the Tabby Persian cats have brilliant copper eye-colour except the Silver Tabby which has green or hazel eyes and the Silver Patched Tabby which has copper or hazel eyes.

TORTOISESHELL PERSIANS are brightly patched in black and red and often have a stripe or blaze right down the centre of their faces. The diluted version of this variety, which is also invariably female due to the effect of a sex-linked gene, is the

17

This composed and very glamorous Blue-Cream Persian is *Dawnstar Dearest Dolly*.

Blue-Cream, with patches of palest blue-grey and light pinkish cream.

The CALICO is a white cat with bright, clearly defined patches of black and red, and the Dilute Calico is white with patches of blue and cream.

Like the Tortoiseshell and Calico, the BI-COLOUR has been around since the turn of this century. It is white with heavy and quite symmetrical patches of colour which may be black, blue, red or cream. The legs, feet, underparts, chest and muzzle should be white, and show judges like to see an inverted 'V' in white, down between the eyes. The Persian Van Bi-color has its black, blue, red or cream markings restricted to the head, tail and legs, while the rest of the cat's long coat is white, and like all the tortoiseshell group, the eyes are brilliant copper.

A rather controversial breed is the PEKE-FACE PERSIAN which is bred in red and in Red Tabby varieties and conforms in colour and body type to the standard of the Red Persian and Red Tabby Persian. The head, however, is quite different, resembling that of a Pekinese dog with a tiny nose often indented between the very large round eyes. In profile, the head is quite flat, and the depressed nose produces a wrinkled effect of the muzzle.

In Britain the Persians are known generally as Long-hairs, and cats of different colours often have slightly different standards of points for show features. The Calico is called the Tortoiseshell and White, and strangely, though the Tortoiseshell Long-hair must be 'patched', its Blue-Cream cousin must have intermingled colours in its coat.

Smithway Jered is an example of a Peke-Face Red Tabby, and comes from a famous line of such cats.

Calico cats are patched in black, red and white. Like *Champion Cotton Patches Holly*, most enjoy home comforts.

19

OTHER LONG-HAIRED BREEDS

There are several other long-coated breeds of cat which, because of different bone structure and body conformation, cannot be classified as Persians. Nevertheless, they are very well established. These include all the Himalayans, the Birman, the Somali, the Balinese, the Turkish Angora and the Maine Coon, plus the Chocolate and Lilac Solid-Colour cats, bred as an off-shoot to the Himalayan breeding programmes. The British registering body does not recognize some of the long-haired breeds – the Peke-Face, the Persian Van Bi-color, the Cream and Blue Tabbies or the Maine Coon, for example – but does have Chocolate Self and Lilac Self Long-hairs, plus their tortoiseshell equivalents, Chocolate Tortoiseshell or Chocolate Cream, and Lilac Tortoiseshell or Lilac-Cream. It knows the Himalayan as the Colourpoint and classes the Somali with the Abyssinian and the Balinese with the Siamese.

HIMALAYAN Himalayan cats are of Persian type, large and chunky, but are coloured only on the 'points' or extremities of the body in the pattern known as Himalayan, and typified by the popular Siamese. These cats were deliberately bred by first crossing Siamese and Persian, and then back-crossing to other long-haired cats over many generations to establish and fix the desired type. The body colour must be pale and even, but slight shading is allowed on older cats which do tend to darken along the flanks. The 'points' are the mask or face (except for the areas above the eyes and between the ears), the legs and feet, and the entire tail. Similar to the Siamese, the varieties are named according to the colour of these points which must all match in the individual cat. The accepted varieties are Seal Point, Blue Point, Chocolate Point, Lilac Point, Flame Point and Blue-Cream Point. All Himalayans have blue eyes.

Above: Also produced by the action of a special genetic factor, two *Marisha* Himalayans show examples of points colour – Blue-Point (left) and Cream-Point (right).

Far left: This little kitten from the *Shimron* cattery shyly hides the stark white paws that label her a Birman.

The Sacred Cat of Burma, or
Birman, has its origins shrouded
in legend. Champion *Shimron
Lucius* is a fine example of this
old breed.

BIRMAN The Birman, or Sacred Cat of
Burma, is said to have descended from
cats which, centuries ago, guarded the
Temple of Lao-Tsun in Burma. Raised in
France during the 1920s, and almost
decimated during the Second World
War, it survived thanks to a few dedicated
breeders and eventually made its way to
Britain. At about the same time two
Tibetan Temple kittens were sent to the
United States and, through exchange of
correspondence, were seen to closely
resemble the Birmans. Breeding stock was
exchanged and the breed is now well
established. The Birman cat is Himalayan
in pattern but its body structure is different, and its head is longer and finer,
sporting a Roman nose. The most distinctive feature of the breed, however, is the
fact that its four dark legs all terminate in

stark white gloves. The Birman may have
Seal, Blue, Chocolate or Lilac points and,
like all the Himalayan-marked breeds, its
eyes are decidedly blue.

ANGORA Turkey, the home of some of the
original long-hairs several centuries ago,
has produced more modern stock for
today's breeders of fancy cats. In 1962 a
pair of cats was brought to the U.S.A.
from the zoo in Ankara, and later, in
1966, to prevent too much interbreeding,
two more were purchased. All the Turkish
imports were white, some with amber eyes
and some with odd eyes. With care in
breeding, and yet more imports, the breed
was formally established by 1970. Today,
the Turkish Angora is accepted in Black,
Blue, Black Smoke, Blue Smoke, Calico,
Bi-colour, and Tabbies of Silver, Brown,
Red or Blue. It is a cat of medium size

Left: *Pr. and Ch. Gnirha's Amy of Derry Downs* is a blue spay of the breed known as the Turkish Angora.

Below: Semi long-haired, the auburn patterned white Van Cat also descends from cats of Turkish stock.

with a wedge-shaped head and long pointed ears furnished with tiny tufts. The coat is very fine and silky, and shows a tendency to wave, especially on the stomach. The hair is of medium length over the body and extra long at the ruff and on the plume-like tail. In the Silver Tabby Turkish, the eye colour may be either green or hazel, but in all other varieties, the eyes should be amber.

The Angora is not recognized in Britain, but its close cousin, known as the Turkish Van, was recognized in 1969. Called the Turkish Van after the district in which it was first discovered, this cat is white with dark auburn markings on the head and tail. It made its way onto the front pages of several newspapers when early imports showed an unusual delight in swimming.

23

MAINE COON The U.S.A.'s native breed is the Maine Coon, a large and very hardy cat, long-coated and with a longish head, big eyes and large, wide-set and heavily tufted ears. First found in the State of Maine, this handsome cat was thought to be the result of crossbreeding between an Angora, landed by a ship from foreign shores, and a raccoon, although it is now known that biologically this was impossible.

Although the original Maine Coons are thought to have been dark tabby with white markings on the chest, the breed today is recognized in several colours. Regardless of coat, the eyes should be either green, gold or copper; the white varieties also allow blue or odd eyes. As well as the normal colours of black, blue, white, red and cream, the Maine Coon may assume any of the Tabby colours, those of the Tortoiseshell group, the Cameo series and the Smokes, the Chinchillas, the Shaded Silver, the Bi-colours and the Calicos. In addition it may be tabby with the addition of white areas on the bib, underparts, all four paws and the face. An active and playful cat, a Maine Coon makes an enjoyable pet.

CARE AND CHARACTER OF THE LONG-HAIRED CATS

In personality the Persian and other long-coated breeds show great variation, some being quiet, staid and dignified, while others clown around, demanding a great deal of attention. Most long coats need very regular and specialized grooming to keep them in perfect condition, and the softer coats tend to form mats and knots if neglected. It is important to train kittens of all long-coated varieties to accept gentle daily brushing and combing, especially under the body and between the fore and hind legs where the softest hair and tenderest areas are to be found. Special grooming powder is available and may be rubbed into the coat to clean it and help separate the hairs, but such powder must be brushed out thoroughly after each application to prevent its ingestion by the cat during its own careful grooming with its rough tongue. The different types of coat require special kinds of combs, but in general the very long- and thick-coated cats should be groomed with a coarse comb, while the slightly shorter or coarser coats may benefit from the use of a fine comb.

Above: Most long-haired varieties, like these Birman kittens, need regular daily grooming.

Far left: *Illya's Yankee Patriot of Roselu* is a large and very handsome example of America's native breed, the Maine Coon.

25

Short-haired Cats

Far right, top: Many self-coloured cats show distinct ghost-tabby markings as very young kittens.

The first short-haired cats were brought to North America by the Pilgrim fathers and other missionary travellers, and helped earn their keep by protecting the early settlers' meagre food supplies from the ravages of rodents. The cats were allowed to roam freely and intermated for many generations producing naturally strong offspring in a wide variety of coat colours and patterns. As more immigrants arrived, so they brought their own cats, and as those with 'true pioneering spirit' headed westwards, their cats went along and so the species spread across the continent. At the beginning of the 20th century, with the growing interest in the keeping of 'fancy' cats, the Domestic Short-hair became established as an official breed group. The very first Short-hair to be registered, according to the records of the Cat Fanciers' Association, was called Champion Belle of Bradford and was described as an Orange Tabby male, from England, born on 1 June 1860. Slowly over the years, selective breeding from the original Domestic Short-hairs produced today's American Short-hair, which conforms to an exacting show standard. The American Short-hair differs from the British Short-hair in several ways; the American Short-hair is generally larger than its British counterpart, with a slightly finer head and longer nose.

THE AMERICAN SHORT-HAIR

Said to be America's only breed of true working cat, the Short-hair is built for survival and self-sufficiency should the need arise. It is lithe, active and very powerful, and therefore makes an efficient hunter. The type selected for breeding and showing has ensured that the face has not become foreshortened, and that the

dentition has been retained as nature intended; in fact, the entire anatomy of the Short-hair has remained that of the ideal small carnivore.

For show purposes, the American Short-hair should have a medium-to-large body with a well-developed chest and strong shoulders. The legs are of medium length with strong bones and muscles and rounded paws. The head is quite large with full cheeks and a square

Far right: Like the Long-hairs, Short-hairs come in a wide range of colours and patterns. Left is a classic Silver Tabby, and right, a Silver Spotted.

muzzle and is topped by wide-set rounded ears. The bright clear eyes should be round and wide and show a slight slant at the outer corners; they should have an alert, questioning expression. The Short-hair's tail is heavy at the base and of medium length with a blunted end and is used constantly to express the animal's moods.

With its short, thick and even-textured coat, the American Short-hair is accepted in a wide range of colours. The White may have either blue, gold or odd-coloured eyes and a pure glistening white coat. The Black must be soundly coloured right through its coal-black coat and must have brilliant gold eyes. In the Blue Short-hair, the lighter shades are preferred, but cats are penalized for showing paler undercoats. The Red Short-hair is a rich deep amber while its dilute cousin, the Cream, must be a uniform shade of pale buff. Like the Black and the Blue, these varieties must have deep golden eyes, and must not show any shading or markings in the coat.

Far right: This superb
American Short-hair proudly
shows off his classic design
etched in black on a sparkling
silver undercoat.

Right: *Belle Bete's Snowman* is a
rare Shaded Silver variety of
American Short-hair.

Far right: In Odd-Eyed White
cats, one eye is blue and the
other gold or copper.

There are Chinchilla Short-hairs and the more heavily marked Shaded Silvers, both with black tipping colouring the ends of the white hairs, producing perhaps the most dramatic varieties of all within the group. Similar to their long-haired brothers and sisters, they have emerald or aquamarine eyes, darkly outlined with black, giving them filmstar looks.

Red tipping colours the Shell and Shaded Cameo Short-hairs' otherwise white coats. The Shell Cameo or Red Chinchilla is quite exquisite, looking like a sparkling, pink-toned puss, while the Shaded's heavier tipping produces the effect of a red mantle over its back. There are three types of Smoke Short-hairs, all with white undercoats and such heavy tipping that the cats look solid-coloured in repose. They are the Black Smoke, the Blue Smoke and the Cameo Smoke.

Parti-coloured Short-hairs are very popular. Those which are white with heavy, unbrindled areas of another colour almost covering their bodies are called Bi-colours and may be Black-and-White, Blue-and-White or Red-and-White. The Tortoiseshell has clear red-and-black patches all over the body, and judges like to see a red blaze bisecting the sometimes bizarre face. Paler and more ethereal is the grey-and-buff patched Blue-Cream Short-hair. The Calico is white with tortoiseshell patching and the Dilute Calico is white with defined markings in blue-grey and buff. Tabby Short-hairs may be Classic patterned or Mackerel striped and come in several colours including Silver, Brown, Blue, Red, Cream and Cameo. There are Patched Tabbies, too, in which the normal markings are interspersed with red or cream patches, producing, in effect, tortoiseshell-tabbies often called 'Torbies'.

The Tortoiseshell, Calico, Blue-Cream, Dilute Calico and all the Torbies are invariably female, due to the effect of

28

the sex-linked red gene, so these have to be mated to males of other varieties to produce kittens of correct colouring. Eye colour for most of these Short-hairs should be brilliant gold: the exceptions are the Silver Patched Tabby which should have gold or hazel eyes, and the Silver Tabby which should have eyes of green or hazel.

THE EXOTIC SHORT-HAIR

Essentially an American breed group of cats, the Exotic Short-hair was deliberately produced by crossing top-class pedigree Persians with American Short-hairs. The aim was to develop a cat with the body conformation and head of the Persian, but with an easy-care type of coat. Eventually, after careful selection of stock and judicious backcrosses, cats of the desired type and coat texture finally emerged, making their official show debut in the 1967–8 season.

The perfect Exotic is of the same type as its Persian ancestors, with a massive

This typical British Blue Short-hair has true blue colouring and the massive frame required by his breed standard.

round head, full cheeks, strong jaws and a determined chin. Its ears are tiny, set far apart and low down on the head so that they almost merge with its contours. The large round eyes are also set wide apart and have a kind, intelligent expression and the nose is of the short, snub kind. The neck is short and thick and the body is chunky with short thick legs and large paws. The tail is quite short and is carried straight, and held lower than the line of the spine. The coat is dense with a plushy texture and, although it is short, stands out from the body in a distinctive way. Exotics may be bred in the same colours as the American Short-hairs and appeal particularly to people who really admire Persians but cannot cope with the care needed to keep the long coat in show condition.

Grooming is comparatively simple, but for show purposes, it is important to ensure that the coat is brushed to stand out from the body, enhancing the cat's generally rounded lines. Those who keep the breed say that their Exotic pets are quiet and well-behaved, playful but rarely destructive and gentle with small children.

THE BRITISH SHORT-HAIR

Although the British Short-hair is said to be the British equivalent of the American Short-hair, it differs in many respects and is accepted as a separate breed at cat shows. When placed side by side, the differences in the two breeds are clear. The British has a very soft and resilient coat, while that of the American's is short, thick and hard. Their heads are distinctive, too; the British cat has an exceptionally round, full-cheeked face with a short broad nose and tiny wide-apart ears, while its American cousin's head is far less extreme. The British Short-hair is recognized for competition in a slightly restricted range of colours, but the most popular variety on both sides of the Atlantic is the British Blue. Massive and generally of exceptionally good type, it should be an even light blue in colour and have huge full copper-coloured eyes. This cat was treated as a separate breed by some associations at first, but is now generally accepted as being merely a colour variety of British Short-hair. Unlike the Exotics, the British and American Short-hairs are usually bred only within their own breed groups and not outcrossed with Persians.

CARE AND CHARACTER OF AMERICAN AND BRITISH SHORT-HAIRS

British and American Short-hairs are alike in temperament, being gentle and quietly inquisitive cats, active and playful but not too demanding of time and attention. The dense coat of the British Short-hair needs regular brushing and combing to remove dead hair, and is generally cleaned with fine grooming

30

powder before show appearances. The characteristic 'bloom' of the healthy Britisher is accomplished more by correct feeding of a good diet than by typical attention to the coat.

OTHER SHORT-HAIRED CATS

CHARTREUX Another blue-coloured short-haired cat is the Chartreux which originated in France several centuries ago, and has always been kept as a true breed. Said to have been developed in the Carthusian monastery of the monks who made Chartreuse liqueur, the breed descended from cats first brought to France from South Africa. Some think the cats could have been named after a special kind of naturally blue-grey wool imported by the French from Spain, and known as 'Pile de Chartreux'. In any case the cat has been known by this name for many years. Buffon, the French naturalist, wrote about cats in his *Natural History* published in 1756, and described the four common sorts as being the Domestic, the Spanish (a tortoiseshell), the Angora and the Chartreux.

In 1970 the first Chartreux cats were imported to the United States and were soon accepted by most associations and recognized as being quite distinct from

Above: A cross-bred Cream kitten enjoying some summer sun.

Left: Most Short-hairs enjoy living as family pets and are easy to maintain in peak condition with very little grooming.

31

Right: This strikingly marked
Calico Short-hair rules the roost
at the *Swady* cattery in Seattle.

Below: *Satin Son Chumash*, a fine
blue Mackerel Tabby American
Short-hair stud male.

the British Blue and the up-and-coming
Exotics. Although some people declare
the Chartreux and the British Blue to be
one and the same breed, there are several
differences between them. The head of the
Chartreux, though broad, is not round
and its nose is short and straight with a
fairly narrow muzzle. The ears are small,
but set quite high on the head and the
large eyes may be of any shade in the
range from pale gold to orange. The
evenly coloured coat is dense and soft and
often appears to have silver highlights.
This cat is bold and interested in every-
thing going on around it, and is said to be
especially good with dogs.

AMERICAN WIRE-HAIR In 1966 a mutation occurred in a litter of domestic cats causing an unusual kitten to be born on a farm in Verona, New York. The kitten was easily distinguished from its brothers and sisters by its strange coat, which consisted of a few sparse and wiry hairs. When an experienced cat breeder heard of the unusual kitten, he took it, along with a plain-coated sister, and began to conduct some breeding tests.

Adam, the original wire-haired kitten, matured and was mated to several American Short-hair queens, as well as to his litter-sister. All produced some wire-haired kittens in their litters. The fact that only one wire-haired parent seemed necessary in order to produce similar offspring showed that the mutant gene was dominant over normal coat type, and enabled outcrosses to be made at each generation.

In 1977 the Cat Fanciers' Association Incorporated granted full championship status to the new breed, now known as the American Wire-hair, allowing it to be shown in all the usual, accepted short-haired varieties' colours. The Wire-hair is a cat of medium size and does not show extremes of type in any feature. The gently rounded lines of the head are pleasing, and it has rather prominent cheeks and a slight break at the whisker pads. The muzzle and chin are strong and the medium-sized ears with slightly rounded tips are set fairly wide apart. The eyes are beautiful, being large and round, bright and clear, with a very alert look. They tilt slightly upwards at the outer corners. The strange and distinctive coat has crimped, bent and hooked hairs, which gives the cat its overall wire-haired appearance, and it is unusually coarse and springy to the touch. Even the hair inside the ears is crimped and the whiskers, also, should be curly.

SPHYNX Another mutation occurred in 1966 which affected the feline coat structure, but this time the phenomenon happened in Ontario, Canada. An ordinary black-and-white house cat produced a litter of kittens in which one kitten was seen to be entirely hairless. As the litter grew up, the little hairless kitten remained virtually nude, but some very

Most Short-hairs make easy-going, undemanding pets, and are quiet companions.

Champion *Calliope Rosey Dawn*, a red tabby-and-white Manx.

landing on the Isle of Man just off the Western coast of England. Another legend links their taillessness with the fact that the island's warriors favoured cat-tail plumes in their helmets so in order to prevent the destruction of her kittens, a mother cat bit off all their tails. Even Noah has been blamed for the denuded rump of the Manx cat. Apparently the pair of cats arrived very late, just as the great Ark was about to set sail. As they came aboard the heavy doors swung shut and cut off their tails.

How the first tailless cat came to live on the Isle of Man is unknown but one can be certain that it found the environment conducive to survival, for tailless kittens were soon seen on farms. The Manx Cat Club was formed in 1901 and the breed began to compete at cat shows.

By 1933 Manx cats had crossed the Atlantic and were causing interest at American shows and, although never seen in large numbers, have remained popular to this day. A true show specimen of the breed gives an overall impression of roundness, having a round head, round muzzle and rounded rump. The body is chunky and powerfully built, and the hind legs are considerably longer than the forelegs. The cheeks are full with pronounced cheekbones and a definite break enhances the rounded whisker pads. The muzzle is well developed, the chin strong, and the ears are wide at the base tapering to slightly rounded tips. The eyes are large and lustrous and set at a slight angle towards the neat nose.

The perfect show Manx is not only totally tailless but has a little dimple at the end of the backbone where the tail would normally be set. This type of Manx cat, with its high round rump, is known as the Rumpy in the island of its birth. Sometimes a Manx cat will have a small rise of bone at the end of the spine, and is then called a Rumpy-riser. Occasionally a very short tail stump may be present, and such Manx cats are called Stubbies in the United States and Stumpies in their homeland. The Longy has a tail which is not full length and some kittens, born of Manx parents, have normal tails but are of Manx configuration otherwise. Due to genetic problems encountered by breeding true Manx together, Risers, Stubbies, Longies and even Tailed Manx are often used to breed with totally tailless mates.

short fine hairs grew on her head, tail and feet, while the rest of the body sprouted some extremely short and sparse down, almost invisible to both sight and touch. From this original kitten, a breed known as the Sphynx was developed. It has remained very rare indeed and has been ignored by many of the official feline bodies.

MANX True Manx cats are unique. They are totally tailless and are said to be the descendants of similar cats which swam ashore from a wrecked Spanish ship,

This has been found more satisfactory than outcrossing to other short hairs as the characteristic Manx head and body conformation is then retained.

Manx cats make charming pets, being gentle and affectionate and good with children. They have quiet voices but will respond when addressed.

SCOTTISH FOLD Just as a rare mutation was responsible for the birth of the first Manx, so another similar phenomenon must have taken place in 1961, when a Scottish shepherd noticed that one of the farm kittens had peculiar ears. Two years later, the same mother cat produced two more 'lop-eared' kittens and the shepherd took one of them into his home, determined to found a new breed. It was eventually proved that the folded effect of the ears

Above: This blue tabby Manx, Penasco's *Sugar 'n' Spice*, has a tiny tuft instead of a tail.

Left: Brown Patched Tabby, or Torbie in colour, this unusual Manx kitten is *Tynwald's Pistol Packin' Mama*.

35

Right: *Capricorn's Gilmour of Swady* is a massive Scottish Fold, first discovered in Scotland but now popular in most of the United States, where it is prized for its uniquely down-turned ears.

Below: Scottish Fold kitten *Swady's Charity of Pickabob* hides coyly in the plants.

was due to the action of a simple dominant gene, and, therefore, even if only one parent showed the trait, some folded-ear kittens would arrive in a litter.

Despite the efforts of its breeders, the British Governing Council of the Cat Fancy refused to recognize the Scottish Fold as a viable and desirable breed, possibly because veterinary opinion stated that they might have hearing difficulties and a natural propensity to diseases of the ear. Close breeding had also produced some kittens with skeletal defects. Eventually, Scottish and English breeders sent their stock to the United States and careful breeding programmes ensured the survival of this unique cat. The Cat Fanciers' Association accepted the Scottish Fold for registration in 1976, and all cats of the breed alive today can have their ancestry traced back to Susie, the mother of the shepherd's cat. The Scottish Fold may be bred in colours similar to those allowed for the American Shorthair and, apart from the ears, is a typical short-haired breed: short and stocky with a strong, round head and large rounded eyes. The unusual ears fold forward and down on the forehead and are set in a caplike fashion which gives a curved silhouette to the top line of the head. The Scottish Fold is a gentle, quiet and sweet-natured cat which makes a delightful and unusual house pet.

Foreign and Oriental Cats

In the Foreign and Oriental group of pedigree cats there are several unusual and attractive breeds, many of which have their own range of colour varieties. Several are named after the countries from which they are said to have originated. Almost all the 'Foreign' cats are short-coated, although there are a few varieties with long hair, and most have long lean bodies, fine bones and narrow pointed heads making them distinct from the American, British, European and Domestic Short-hairs.

ABYSSINIAN Called 'children of the gods', their many admirers consider them to have descended from the sacred cats of Ancient Egypt. In fact, an Abyssinian-type cat was brought out of Abyssinia, now known as Ethiopia, in 1868. She was taken to England but it is not known for certain whether or not she was responsible for founding the breed in that country. By 1882 Abyssinian cats were recognized for show purposes in England, and were similar to today's cat of the same breed. During the 1890s their name was constantly changed and they were known variously as Russians, Spanish, Hare Cats, Bunny Cats and British Ticked. It was in 1906 that the first Abyssinians were imported to the United States from England, and gradually the breed developed successfully on both sides of the Atlantic into the distinctive and stylish cat that graces the leading shows of today. The American Cat Fanciers' Association recognizes the Abyssinian in its usual colour, known as Ruddy, and in an alternative variety known as Red. In Britain, however, breeders have also produced kittens in blue, chocolate, lilac, cream and silver, although not all the varieties are officially recognized by the Governing Council of the Cat Fancy.

The Abyssinian is a lithe and sinuous cat with a heart-shaped head and large wide-apart ears, often sporting lynx-like tufts at the tips. Its eyes are almond-shaped, large, bright and very expressive, and either gold or green in colour. It has a slender body and slim legs. The tail, though thick at the base, is long and tapers to a point. It is the coat, however, that makes the Abyssinian different from all other cats. The texture is soft, fine, silky and fairly short, and each hair is clearly

Asking to be rescued from a high perch is a brightly coloured Red or Sorrel Abyssinian kitten.

Right: The Abyssinian is thought by some to closely resemble the sacred cats of the Ancient Egyptians.

Below: A long-haired version of the Abyssinian is known as the Somali, represented here by one of the *Rainkey* kittens.

marked with two or three bands of dark colour. This imparts a distinctive ticked appearance to the entire coat. The Ruddy Abyssinian is richly brown with darker brown or black ticking; the undercoat is orange-brown; and the tip of the tail, the eyelids and the paw pads are black. The Red Abyssinian is sometimes called Sorrel, and is a warm glowing red, with ticking of chocolate-brown. The eyelids, the tips of the ears and tail, and the paw pads are also chocolate-brown, giving a glowing effect to the whole cat. The show Abyssinian is faulted for having any tabby markings or bars of dark colour on the ticked coat, or any white areas other than its naturally pale chin.

Easy to groom, quiet-voiced, clean and tidy, this is an ideal breed for the discerning owner. Like most other Foreign cats, however, the Abyssinian likes the company of its own kind and responds best to quiet, gentle attention. Though sometimes shy with strangers, Abyssinian cats are very affectionate towards their owners and prove to be highly intelligent, easily trained pets.

SOMALI Some of the very early Abyssinian cats carried the recessive factor for producing long coats in their genetic make-up, but only when two such 'carriers' were intermated was there a chance of long-coated kittens being born. Over the years breeders occasionally reported the appearance of such kittens but it was not until comparatively recently that the long-coated Abyssinian was developed as a separate breed and christened the Somali.

Identical to the normal Abyssinian in all respects except in the length of its coat, the Somali may be either Ruddy or Red. At birth the kittens are heavily marked and rather dark, but as the fur grows and the kitten coat moults out, the ticked effect begins to show. The coat is very soft to the touch, dense, but very fine in texture. It is of medium length over the body and flanks, slightly shorter over the shoulders, longer on the ruff and trousers, and gives a full, brush-like look to the tail. Even the ears have long hair with horizontal tufts reaching right across the inner apertures. Alert, nimble and inquisitive, the Somali has a temperament similar to its Abyssinian brothers and sisters, but the coat needs a little more care, with a daily comb through, paying special attention to the soft hair under the body, between the legs and behind the ears. Originally developed exclusively in the United States, the Somali finally achieved full championship status from the Cat Fanciers' Association in 1978, and cats of the breed have since been exported to England and other parts of Europe. In Australia and New Zealand, long-coated Abyssinians also appeared in litters from time to time and careful breeding soon established the Somali in those countries.

BURMESE In 1930 a retired ship's doctor, who bred cats for a hobby, left his home for a trip to Burma. During his visit he was given an unusual little cat called Wong Mau, who resembled a dark Siamese. Back home in San Francisco, Wong Mau settled down, and was eventually mated to a Siamese. Her litter consisted of some normal Siamese-coloured kittens and some darker ones just like herself. Eventually the dark kittens were mated together and produced even darker offspring with glossy coats. These kittens were destined to be the ancestors of the breed now known as Burmese.

Although granted recognition in 1936, the Burmese cat's charter was withdrawn in 1947 because the Cat Fanciers' Association was concerned by reported bad breeding practices. However, the Burmese Cat Society worked hard for their breed, and status was eventually restored in 1953. During the suspension some Burmese cats were sent to England to introduce the breed to the British cat fanciers. It has proved immensely popular, although of slightly different type to the American Burmese of today.

All the original Burmese cats were a rich dark brown colour, now known as Sable in the U.S.A. and Brown in Great Britain, and this colour is considered by many to be the only 'true' colour for the breed. Dilute and recessive genes lurked within the original cats, however, and

Chocolate Burmese like this one arose quite spontaneously from normal Sable stock.

blue, chocolate and lilac kittens arrived, from time to time, in otherwise normal litters.

Of medium size, the Burmese is substantially built and feels surprisingly heavy for its size. It should be very hard and muscular and must never be allowed to become obese.

The head of the American show Burmese should be rounded without any flat planes, either full face or in profile, and must have a distinct dip below the eyes. The ears are of medium size, set wide apart and tilted slightly forward, and the eyes are also wide with rounded apertures and can vary in colour from yellow to gold. In England the breed is accepted in Brown, Blue, Chocolate, Lilac, Red, Cream and four shades of Tortoiseshell; the head and eye shape differ slightly from those of its American cousin which are broaders and rounder respectively.

In addition to the Sable Burmese, other colours are seen at some American shows. The chocolate-coloured cat is known as Champagne Burmese; there is a Blue variety; and a lilac-coloured one is called a Platinum Burmese. Whatever their colour, Burmese cats all share the same sort of short, fine, glossy coat, with a satin-like texture. It needs very little grooming to keep it in perfect condition, benefiting most from daily grooming with clean, dry hands. Burmese cats are very affectionate and love to be held or to sit high on their

Above: Grand Champion *Sidarka Henry Hotfoot*, Sable or Brown Burmese.

Right: Rare and beautiful dilute Burmese kittens appear from time to time in planned litters. Here we have (left to right) Lilac or Platinum, Lilac-Tortie and Blue-Tortie youngsters.

40

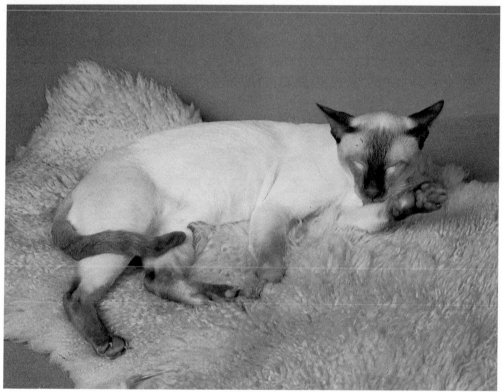

Above: Once called the Royal Cats of Siam, Seal Points remain the most popular colour in that breed.

Left: Chocolate Point Siamese retain their pale ivory coats throughout life and have deep brown points.

47

both blue and chocolate genes intermated and a fourth colour became apparent. Like a very pale ethereal blue-pointed cat was the elusive Lilac Point, called Frost Point by some bodies.

Siamese cats soon became one of the most popular breeds in the world. They are very extroverted and talkative and make magnificent pets for people who expect two-way relationships with their animals. If ignored or neglected the Siamese can become morose and neurotic and may develop bad habits such as fur pulling or stropping the furniture. Given proper care, affection and companionship – human, feline or even canine – the Siamese can be the best house pet of all.

The ideal Siamese is dainty and svelte with a long body, fine long legs and a thin tapered tail. Its head should be long and wedge-shaped with straight lines from all angles. Its large ears should advance and follow the lines of the head. Its eyes are very Oriental and of deep vivid blue. The Seal Point has a pale fawn body and deep seal-brown points. The Blue Point is bluish white of a cold tone, and deep slate grey on the points. The Chocolate Point has an ivory body and warm-toned milk-chocolate points. The Lilac Point is glacial white with pinkish, frosty grey points. The coat texture is very short and fine, lying close to the body and is very easy to keep in top show condition. Hand grooming imparts a healthy glow, and a firm buffing with a silk cloth provides the finishing touch.

Breeders of Siamese cats decided to increase the range of colour varieties by adding red and tabby genes to their pointed cats. This was done by cross-mating, in the initial stages, to pedigree Short-hairs of the desired colours. As was expected, this resulted in loss of Foreign type and Himalayan patterning in the first litters. Careful back-crosses were made to top-quality Siamese, and eventually the new colour varieties emerged.

In England all such cats are considered Siamese and have standards identical to those of the four basic, natural varieties. They are known as Tabby Pointed (of all colours), Red Pointed, Cream Pointed and Tortie Pointed (again in four basic colours). In the United States, however, such cats are known as Colorpoint Short-hairs and the tabby-pointed cats are called Lynx Point, and may be Seal, Blue, Chocolate or Lilac. The Red Point is known as Red-Lynx Point and the four tortoiseshell varieties are called Seal-Tortie Point, Blue-Cream Point, Chocolate-Cream Point and Lilac-Cream Point respectively.

Red Point Siamese cats are known as Red Colorpoint Short-hairs by most American registration bodies. Like all Siamese they have beautiful blue eyes.

BALINESE Occasionally a long-coated kitten was born in an otherwise normal Siamese litter, and in the 1940s a breeder in California and another in New York decided to start a serious programme for breeding such cats as a separate variety. Of identical type to their short-coated Siamese cousins, these long-coated, pointed cats were named Balinese, their graceful movements and daintiness reminding their pioneering breeders of the beautiful dancers of Bali.

The exquisite Balinese must not be confused with the Himalayan, although both have long coats and both have Siamese colouring. The Himalayan is a true Persian cat with colour only on its points, while the Balinese is a true Siamese cat with long hair. The Balinese coat is easy to comb through daily, keeping it tangle-free. Playful, acrobatic and energetic, Balinese cats make good pets, but should not be left alone or allowed to become bored. They seem to love dogs, especially the large breeds, and get along very well with children. Recognized colours include Seal Point, Blue Point, Chocolate Point and Lilac Point which correspond to the same varieties in Siamese, and experimental matings have been conducted with the object of producing other colours.

Balinese are long-coated Siamese cats. Here (right) is a lilac-pointed Balinese accompanied by a blue-pointed, short-coated Balinese Variant.

ORIENTAL SHORT-HAIRS are manmade varieties produced by removing the 'pointed' pattern from Siamese cats while retaining the very elegant, fine Foreign bone structure and conformation. Therefore, all the Oriental Short-hairs are, in effect, self-coloured Siamese cats. In England similar cats are known as either Foreign or Oriental Short-hairs, the prefix 'Foreign' being appended to cats with solid-coloured coats, while the prefix 'Oriental' is used for non-solid colours such as spotted, tabby, tortoiseshell and smoke. Orientals come in an amazing selection of colours. The solids may be White with blue eyes, Ebony, Blue, Chestnut, Lavender, Red or Cream. The Shaded colour group includes Silver and Cameo, while the Smokes may be Ebony, Blue, Chestnut, Lavender or Cameo. Tabbies can be marked in four patterns – the Classic, the Mackerel, the Spotted or the Ticked – and the markings, which all appear on lighter base coats, can be Ebony, Blue, Chestnut, Lavender, Red or Cream. In the Silver Tabby, it is the base coat which is silver, and the markings are black, while in Cameo Tabbies, the off-white base coat is covered with red markings. Oriental Parti-colours include Tortoiseshell, Blue-Cream, Chestnut Tortie and Lavender-Cream. In all colour varieties, green eye-colour is preferred, but amber may also be permitted.

Most Oriental Short-hairs are lively, inquisitive and highly entertaining. These are Oriental Spotted kittens.

51

Breeders, selecting suitable stock for the development of Oriental Short-hairs, attached great importance to features such as health and temperament, as well as good looks and desired colours and patterns. This has resulted in a very strong, healthy breed group. The cats are easy to handle and groom and make ideal house pets.

EGYPTIAN MAU An Oriental Short-hairs was bred in England in an attempt to recreate scientifically the cat deified by the Ancient Egyptians. A careful study of mummified cat remains and artifacts was made and a breeding programme drawn up to produce a fine-boned spotted tabby cat, bronze in colour and with a clearly defined mark, similar to a sacred scarab beetle, neatly etched between the animal's ears. Breeding Siamese with tabbies and other cats of suitable shape and colour, the Egyptian cat eventually emerged, but could only be registered as part of the Oriental group, as the Chocolate variety of the Oriental Spotted Tabby.

In the United States genuine Egyptian cats were imported in 1957. These were much stockier in build than the 'Egyptians' of England, and careful breeding and selection for clear spotting soon produced an acceptable breed, called the Egyptian Mau. 'Mau' is the Ancient Egyptian word for 'cat', and may also be translated as 'to see'. Of medium size, falling midway between that of the Siamese and the Short-hair, the Egypti Mau is muscular and active. The head is a modified wedge with no angular planes, and it has large, slightly pointed ears and slanting almond eyes of light apple green.

The coat pattern should be clearly defined on the body, the legs are barred and the tail banded. There is a characteristic 'M' on the forehead and frown marks which extend between the ears. Accepted colours are the Silver which has charcoal markings on a silver base coat, Bronze which has dark brown markings on a light bronze-coloured base, and Smoke which has dark charcoal-grey markings on a silver undercoat.

Far left: This stylish Oriental or Foreign White queen is Grand Champion *Nomis So-Lareta*.

Below: The silver variety of Egyptian Mau has clear black markings on a bright silver base coat.

JAPANESE BOBTAIL A natural breed which originated in Japan centuries ago is now well known on the American show scene. It was introduced in 1968 and had gained full championship status with the Cat Fanciers' Association by 1976. The Japanese Bobtail is an elegant cat of medium size. It has a long lean body and stands high on slender, muscular legs. It has a long triangular head with high cheekbones and a distinct break at the whisker pads. The ears are large and set rather high on the head, and the eyes are oval in shape and very expressive. As its name suggests, this cat has a most unusual tail. It is very short and rigidly kinked, and is covered with thick fine hair, giving the effect of a pom-pon.

In Japan tri-coloured Bobtail cats of

Above: Two silver Egyptian Mau kittens share a cosy wicker sleeping basket.

Right: A Japanese Bobtail with the typical Mi-ke coat coloration plays happily at *Swady's* cattery.

54

black, red and white are highly prized and are called '*Mi-ke*' (pronounced mee-kay). Breeders of the Bobtail prefer either this coat pattern or bi-coloured cats which may, in turn, produce tri-coloured offspring. In both bi-colour and tri-colour cats, any colour may predominate, but bold patches and contrasting colours are much in demand.

Said to be a very outward going, playful and inquisitive cat, the Bobtail repays early loving care and a happy environment by supplying ideal companionship. It is said to enjoy swimming in the bathtub, and may be taught to retrieve small toys or balls. Talkative in its expressive chirruping little voice, the Japanese Bobtail hates to be left alone, and prefers the company of other Bobtails to cats of different breeds. The coat, which is soft and silky, and short-to-medium in length, is simple to keep in good condition with

very little grooming. The hair grows slightly longer over the stumpy tail.

REX cats resulted from spontaneous and quite separate mutations in ordinary domestic short-hairs, which caused dramatic changes to take place in the structure of their coats. It was in England that the first Rex was recorded. In 1950 on a farm in the county of Cornwall, a kitten with a tightly curled coat was found nestling among its normal-coated littermates. This kitten became the founder of the breed known as Cornish Rex. In 1953 a curly kitten was born to a normal domestic cat in the State of Ohio, and in 1957 a black curly-coated female was adopted by a doctor in Germany. In 1960 another curly kitten was discovered in Devonshire, England, the county bordering Cornwall, but breeding tests soon showed that this cat's curls were due to a

Champion *Garchell Dopey Dreamer*, just Dopey to his many fans, is a blue-coated Devon Rex cat.

totally different gene from the one responsible for the Cornish cat. This second English strain was named the Devon Rex. Incidentally breeding the two strains together produced only plain-coated kittens.

Before long the Rex genes were added to cats of all colours and patterns. In 1979 the Cat Fanciers' Association recognized that there were two quite distinct varieties of Rex cats. Of foreign conformation, both varieties of Rex cats stand high on their long legs. They have elegant bodies, slender necks and long, tapered tails. The head of the Cornish Rex is one-third longer than it is wide with a flat skull and large, high-set ears and oval-shaped eyes. The coat is short and plushy and curls, waves or ripples along the back. The Devon Rex has a full-cheeked face and very large low-set ears. It has a short muzzle and a strongly marked stop below the large oval eyes. Its coat is extremely short and fine, and softly waves rather than curls. It is often slightly longer on the points. Rex cats are penalized for having any bare areas or shaggy patches in the coat.

56

Cat Care

As we have seen in our study of the breeds, pedigree cats are available in all colours and patterns. They can have long, medium, short or curled fur, and can be short and stocky, long and rangy or built somewhere between those two extremes. Cats can have peculiarities such as folded ears, bobtails, or even no tails. But despite all their differences, they remain essentially pet cats, retaining their air of independence and their often-inscrutable charm. Cats without pedigrees can also make delightful pets, and may even be entered in special sections at cat shows. Whether or not they have a known and recorded ancestry, all cats need the same basic care plus a great deal of love and attention.

GROOMING

Grooming your cat should be thought of as a pleasant activity rather than a chore, and it has been recently proven that such grooming and stroking has a beneficial effect on humans, reducing blood pressure and helping to prevent heart disease. Although the very long-coated cats need special combs depending on their type of hair and Rex cats need very soft brushes, basic grooming is merely a matter of commonsense. The object is to brush or comb the animal right through its coat, starting at the head and finishing at the tip of the tail. You must make sure not to miss any areas, particularly those which may matt or form

Most cats make caring and naturally protective mothers.

tangles, such as the soft regions between the legs and the fine hair behind the ears. Grooming powder may be massaged into the coats of long-haired cats, left for a while to absorb grease and dust, and then brushed out thoroughly. Powder may be used to clean some of the short-hairs, too, and very fine-coated breeds, like Siamese, may have a little spray of a proprietary grooming solution applied to their fur.

For show purposes, of course, it is essential to learn to groom your cat expertly, to make it look its very best and to enhance its chances of winning the top awards. Most breeders are pleased to help novice exhibitors who have purchased show kittens, for it is in their own interests to produce winning stock. Sometimes it is necessary to bath a cat, and most felines accept this indignity as long as the water is comfortably hand-hot, shampoo is kept well away from the eyes and the whole

procedure is carried out calmly and quickly. After bathing, the cat must be thoroughly rinsed, or it may lick harmful substances left in its coat, then it should be dried as quickly as possible using thick warm towels. If it does not object too strongly, an electric hair drier can be used.

FEEDING

Correct feeding is of prime importance to a cat and results in a healthy bright-eyed and glossy-coated pet. Food may be canned, fresh, dried or semi-moist and fed raw or cooked, but it is generally best to provide a very varied, well-balanced diet, high in protein and with some crunchy biscuit and strips of fairly tough raw meat to keep the teeth in good order. Fresh clean water should be available at all times even if the cat rarely seems to drink,

Kittens like to have their own private places to which they may retire for a quick wash and rest after meals.

Natural hunters, cats really enjoy the freedom of the garden, but should be confined to the home in towns.

and if you feed a cat a proper diet, there is absolutely no need to add extra vitamins and minerals, although some cats like such pills as treats or rewards for good behaviour. Never feed cats food straight from the refrigerator; always allow it to reach room temperature before offering it to your cat. If you feed your cat any scraps from your own meals, be sure that you remove any sharp pieces of bone of shell from poultry, fish or shellfish.

A PRIVATE PLACE

Every cat should have its own personal bed to which it may retreat whenever it wants to be alone, whether or not it wants to sleep. When a cat retires to its own little haven it should be left in peace. Beds may be made of old cartons, or may be purchased in all manner of materials from plastics to wickerwork and lined in anything from calico to mink. The best beds are easily cleaned and draught-proof, and

should be sited in a place of the cat's own choosing.

Cats also have a natural need to strop the scale from their claws and it is important to teach them to use an acceptable scratching post in preference to the best armchairs. Such lessons must be instilled from an early age, and once learned are rarely forgotten.

CLEAN HABITS

The cat must be trained to use its own litter-tray too. This is quite easy as cats are naturally clean and fastidious creatures. The only time your cat is likely to use some other spot is if you allow the litter to become unacceptably soiled or wet. Very well-designed toilet trays complete with removable covers are available. They have a hole at one end to allow the cat access, and the lid lifts off so that soiled and wet litter can be regularly scooped out for disposal. The tray should be washed regularly with hot water and detergent and then sterilized with a suitable disinfectant, taking care to check that the disinfectant is not harmful to cats. Many disinfectants, even those which are safe for human babies, are highly toxic to cats, causing convulsions and even death, so it is important to stock the home with suitable products when you have pets. The same care should be taken with the cat's food and water bowls. Wash them carefully after each meal, rinse thoroughly under running water and allow to drain dry naturally.

HOW TO CHOOSE AND LOOK AFTER A KITTEN

When buying a kitten, whether it is pedigree or pet quality, you should make sure that you choose one which is healthy and properly weaned. The kitten should be about 12 weeks of age, if possible, before it is taken away from the comfort of its accustomed environment and the companionship of its littermates. You should enquire whether or not the kitten has received any vaccinations against such diseases as Feline Infectious Enteritis, Panleukopaenia, or any of the Upper Respiratory Diseases such as Rhino-tracheitis and Calicivirus, and whether or not the parents have been recently tested as free from Feline Leukaemis Virus.

When checking over the kitten you choose, examine the fur carefully. It should be clean and fresh-looking, without any signs of parasitic infection or fun-gus disease. There should be no scabs or scratches on the skin, or any of the tiny grits which are excreted by cat fleas. Look inside the ears; they should be clean and sweet smelling with a slightly moist appearance. Again, dark grits indicate the presence of parasites, this time of tiny mites which infest the inner ear canals. Check the area under the tail. It should look clean and tidy with no yellow staining to indicate diarrhoea. The kitten's eyes should be bright and clear; the third eyelids should not protrude at

Below: Tiny kittens may be rather apprehensive and need a safe place in which to hide.

Left: Whenever possible, have two kittens rather than one. They will remain playmates for life and healthy competition ensures clean plates at mealtimes.

the inner corners; and there should be no sign of any soreness or discharge. The nostrils, too, should be clean and dry. The young kitten should be playful – unless you call during cat-nap time – and should move properly in a co-ordinated manner. Although its body should feel firm, the stomach should not be distended as this could indicate infestation with intestinal worms.

Some pedigree kittens have slight defects which preclude them from possible championship wins at shows, and you may decide to buy such a kitten at a suitably reduced price. These defects range from mismarking, when the only fault is in the distribution of the coat colours or faulty patterning, to having a knot or kink in the tail. Naturally, such kittens make perfectly healthy pets.

If your new kitten has not had its injections, you must arrange with a veterinary surgeon to take care of these without further delay.

Provide a cosy box for your acquisition, and, whenever possible, have two kittens rather than one, for they will perform a miracle of mathematics, providing you with four times the fun you would get from just one. With two kittens there is natural competition for food and attention, and the young animals develop more quickly and far more fully than similar kittens kept in isolation. Provide your kitten or kittens with plenty of toys, warmth, a good diet, fed in four small daily meals, and your pet will grow strong and healthy in leaps and bounds.

NEUTERING

Unless it is your intention to breed cats, when you will have bought a special queen of top quality from a bona fide breeder, have your pet neutered. If it is a male it is best to arrange castration at about six to eight months of age. The operation is simple and is carried out under a general anaesthetic with no adverse after effects. The kitten generally stays in the hospital for one night and on his return home the next day, plays happily as though nothing had happened. Male cats, left entire, can be very anti-social in their habits, spraying foul-smelling urine all around their homes and territory.

Your kittens need a warm comfortable bed of some sort, and may even settle for an antique cradle!

They love to pick fights if allowed out, and go looking for receptive females. The neutered male is a delight, loving and generally clean around the house, and may still be shown if you wish for there are special classes and top show awards for neutered cats.

Female cats are altered by the operation called spaying which involves an internal operation called an ovariohysterectomy. It is probably best carried out when the kitten is about six months of age, and she is kept at the hospital overnight in order to recover completely from the anaesthetic. When she comes home she will have two or three stitches closing the small incision, and these are generally removed about one week later. Most cats play happily the day after their operation, unless they are queens which have had a litter or two, when they need a little more post-operative rest.

The great outdoors is full of adventure for the curious cat who soon learns to make friends all round.

Troy, a large ginger neuter, typifies the pet cat with his clear bright eyes, glossy coat and alert interested expression.

DAILY MAINTENANCE

Pet cats need very little maintenance apart from daily meals and the correct grooming for their particular sort of coat. Ears and teeth should be checked regularly. Waxy deposits can be lifted from inside the ear flaps with dry cotton buds, and teeth usually keep clean and free from tartar if a few crunchy cat biscuits are given daily. If your cat has bad breath or problems with its teeth, take it to the veterinary office for a check-up. Vaccinations need yearly or two-yearly booster injections and if you show or breed, it is important to institute a regular regime of blood tests and checks for the serious feline diseases. Always check your cat's coat for the presence of parasites and treat fleas without delay before they can become a problem. Some cats suffer from intestinal worms, and if you suspect these, take a sample of your pet's faeces and have it analyzed.

Always remember, provide your cat with its simple requirements and it will remain contented, fit and happy.